# RADICAL
# RESCUE

## T. MARIE SPENCER

PAGE PUBLISHING
Conneaut Lake, PA

First originally published by Page Publishing 2023

ISBN 978-1-6624-8078-2 (pbk)
ISBN 978-1-6624-8079-9 (digital)

Printed in the United States of America

# CONTENTS

# CHAPTER 1

## The Call

My husband and I were minding our own business. While trying to survive marriage, parenting, and working, a most unusual interruption happened.

The phone rang… I answered, "Hello?"

The voice replied with a gentle quiver, "Hello, is this Tara?"

I replied, "Yes, it is."

The man stated, "This is your dad, Kevin."

My heart was pounding, and all the feelings of insecurity, fear, curiosity, and excitement clashed together as I anticipated why he was calling me.

My father Kevin began to explain his reason for calling me, "I have been trying to find you for a while, and your mother gave me your number. The only reason I had the nerve to call you is to let you know that you are royalty!"

While he is talking to me, I am thinking to myself, "Wow… I am talking to my dad!"

He went on to say, "We are the last generation to receive an inheritance from our English ancestors. A prince from England was sent to America to purchase land, oil and waterfront in Kentucky, and we are next to inherit it. Peanut… I want you to be included in the inheritance! You didn't know you were royalty, did you?"

As intriguing as this all sounded, his voice sounded like Charlie Brown's teacher speaking…blah, blah, blah! I dreamed of this day all of my life so it didn't matter to me why he was calling, only that he called.

1

Let me explain my past a little…

My dad left my mom when I was four. I can remember sitting in the front seat of his pickup truck while he was flipping through his pictures of women in his wallet. He leaned over toward me and asked me, "Which one is the prettiest?" I was a Daddy's girl so any little moment of time with him was etched in my memory. Shortly after, he moved away.

He called me Peanut because I was born two months premature. A miracle baby for 1964. The doctors said I would be blind from the incubator and have many allergies. Neither happened.

My mom was sixteen when she had me. Dad was eighteen. They were very poor and had no support. Needless to say, their marriage did not last, and I was left without a dad, and my mom, doing her best, worked all the time.

Because I longed for my father while growing up, I was looking for him in the men I dated. Dark hair, hardworking, and outdoorsy was always my type.

My first husband fits this description. I met him in a local bar at the age of twenty-four. Our dating life lasted three months before I realized I was pregnant. We had a son named Josh, who was born in December of 1989. We were married after Josh was born, but it lasted only two years.

*Vacation Hookup*

Four years later, I met my second husband named Paul. To give you a picture of more detail, at this time, I was a very successful hairstylist, living in a northern suburb of Indianapolis. I was living large with lots of free time to travel, trustworthy babysitters, and a wild and crazy traveling partner named Chloe.

Chloe and I worked together, partied together and traveled at least twice a year together. She was my opposite; tall, blonde and slender with a magnetic personality, and I was petit, brunette, and very quiet. We rarely attracted the same type of man therefore jealousy was not a problem.

Club Med is an all-inclusive vacation spot for singles that included a variety of activities such as water skiing, sailing, tennis, horseback riding, snorkeling, and lots of eating, drinking, and dancing. Chloe, her friend Melanie and myself planned our getaway together with the hard and fast rule, "No phone numbers, no last names, and *no* long-distance relationships!"

On one of our crazy vacations to Club Med, Cancun, we met a group of good-looking guys which were Paul, his cousin Joe, and a friend named Mike. Little did I know, this was going to be a life-changing interaction.

*Paul's Perspective*

Maybe I should chime in here. Joe and I were very close and spent many weekends together enjoying—water skiing, car racing, lots and lots of drinking, and of course, girls.

A year prior, I went on vacation with Joe and Mike, and we had a blast. It was a Florida beach getaway in February, and yes, I met someone, and she followed me home. That turned into a disaster for everyone involved.

So we also developed a hard and fast rule, "No phone numbers, no last names, *no* long-distance relationships, and if we see you with the same girl more than once...*to* the wood shed we go!"

Funny how the girls from the Midwest and guys from New England made the same deal before going on this trip. Wisdom should follow experience. We started drinking the day before we left Boston after a long work week. It was setting out to be a real bender, if you know what I mean. We showed up Saturday morning in Cancún with no sleep and a good buzz—leftover from the night before. We were ready to water ski, sail, wind surf, drink, dance, and pick up girls.

*Meeting Paul*

There he was, sitting on the edge of the dock, dangling his ski in anticipation of the boat coming to retrieve him for his long-awaited to waterski. He had the thickest, dark hair I had ever seen. Then I heard the loudspeaker call, "Paul!" It was the dock overseer calling him to get into position for the boat to pull him. My name was right after his in the lineup, so I quickly put my skis on and dangled them off the edge. I was so nervous to waterski in the ocean because watersports were not my forte. (Therefore, it usually involved a lot of liquid courage.)

## Paul's Input

I had been waterskiing since I was six years old and was quite accomplished. Joe and I competed with a waterski show team. We loved everything fast and dangerous. Plus it was a great way to show off and meet girls. We specifically went to this resort because they offered waterskiing. The one thing I wasn't counting on was skiing with the crocodiles. It sure "ups" your performance quota to know that your next wipeout could be your last. No big deal, I love a challenge.

I noticed Tara on the dock in line after me. I tried to spark some conversation with her but she was pretty quiet. She was pretty good looking but had that I'm-not-interested look on her face. I thought, "Yeah, no thanks. I came here to have some fun, not work for it, if you know what I mean.

## Back to Tara

My turn came and off the dock I skied. Wobbly, I made it back in one piece. Whew! As we were getting ready to head back to the main resort, I noticed Paul sitting on the dock in his colorful wet suit. He was taking in the sun with his head leaning back and eyes closed. It made me think, "I wish I was that comfortable in my own skin."

A little later that day, after we all returned to the main resort, Chloe, Melanie, and I were sitting in the pool lounge at a small round café-style table. Paul came strolling by and boldly slammed his pack of cigarettes on our table, pulled up a chair, and inquired, "Hey, how's it going?" I immediately struggled inside with his personality because I was not buzzed enough to handle his self-confidence. Quickly, I stood up and headed toward the bar for some liquid courage.

*Paul's Comment*

We all went overboard with the "liquid courage" on a regular basis. Drinking takes us from being "risk takers" to being "stupid risk takers." If nothing else, we figured "girls notice the crazies," ha, ha! We started drinking the day before we left and were determined to keep the "buzz going" the entire week.

*According to Tara*

Chloe was checking out Paul's cousin, Joe. All three of them were handsome, Portuguese men who were very friendly, outgoing, and athletic. Joe was the most approachable.

As conversation and small talk had come to an end, I noticed that Paul had the most perfect "flat top" hairstyle I had ever seen. By now, I had enough liquid courage to ask a really bold question, "Do you mind if I touch the top of your head? I have never seen hair as thick as yours, and I'm a hair-stylist."

"Sure, go ahead," as he shrugged his shoulders.

With all boldness, I proclaimed, "Oh wow! I have never felt hair as thick as yours. I could never marry you because I would have to cut your hair every two weeks!"

With confidence Paul replied, "You won't have to worry about that!"

Everyone just chuckled as we walked away to our next adventure.

*Paul*

That night (Sunday), we got really drunk—I mean barf all over the room drunk. How embarrassing! The hotel staff had such a mess to clean up. Joe and Mike seemed to do just fine but I lost my lunch… All night! The next morning, we signed up for the snorkeling trip. This is supposed to be a calm water event in the ocean, but you just never know. We were really hungover, and so were these girls that we just met.

The captain told us that if you are really hungover, you are better off in the water than in a rocking boat. In we jumped! Melanie and Mike didn't come on the dive boat but Joe and I did. Immediately Joe and Chloe were hanging out. They were laughing together like old friends while I was trying not to barf again especially in front of this girl Tara. I jumped in the water where I am very comfortable and so did Tara but she was not confident at all—I mean at all!

She was terrified and it was hard to snorkel because the white caps of the waves would cover the tube. My hangover seemed to wane and this Tara girl needed rescuing. I mean she was freaking out! I said to her, "Just hold on behind me, grab my neck, and I'll swim for us both."

She didn't hesitate for a second. She grabbed me so tight around the neck. It was hard to breathe. (Remember: Mask and snorkel, no life jacket, both of us very hungover, and trying not to add sea sick to the list.) I started swimming with her on my back, and it made me feel like her hero. She was panicking and pushing me underwater, trying to keep her head up but I thought, "If I have to die, saving this chick is an okay way to go." When they said that it was time to go, we all got back in the boat and headed for the shore. It ended on the dock with, "Maybe we'll see you later?"

That's how this sort of thing goes. Young adults hanging out on vacation with no ties or obligations, just free to come and go. Pretty cool.

*Back to Tara*

That evening after dinner, the girls and I were hanging out at the pool-side lounge, having drinks and mingling with the crowd, when low and behold, Paul, Joe, and Mike came strolling in. I immediately made myself disappear into the crowd because I didn't want to be paired up with Paul. As I was trying to strike up conversation with some random guy, Joe came up behind me and scooped me up in his arms to carry me over to Paul. Before he put me down, Paul lifted my shirt to expose my belly, proceeded to lick my stomach, shook salt over it, licked it off, and took a shot of tequila. (They call this a body shot.) Wow! I was stunned to say the least, however, it broke the ice for me.

Needless to say, we were well on our way to cutting loose, and it was time to head over to the beach bar for the nightly dance party.

Yay, I love to dance! As we were all walking to the beach area, the alcohol was kicking in, so I was loosening up, and Paul was not so intimidating to me.

*Paul*

As we walked from the bar to the dance party, Joe and I pulled down our shorts and started jumping around like pogo sticks. We were about thirty feet in front of the girls, laughing our heads off.

*Tara's thoughts*

I started to notice how attractive and funny Paul was. Shots of tequila went down as soon as we entered the bar and my crazy side came out. I grabbed Paul's face and spontaneously locked lips with him passionately just because I felt like it. Then I pulled him out on the dance floor. As I am dancing, I'm thinking to myself, "He is a great kisser and dancer. This guy is refreshingly fun and attractive!"

*Paul's comments*

Some things are scheduled, some things are planned. This just seemed to happen naturally.

A kiss from a beautiful girl that I thought didn't like me, then wanting to dance. Let's just say, the evening is looking up. Wow, this Tara is really pretty—hot actually—and dances really well. We all had a pretty good buzz going. We're in another country with great music, great friends—Joe and Mike—and having a total blast.

*'ira's surprise*

Having the time of my life, dancing, and feeling far from reality, Joe danced over to Paul and whispered something in his ear.

I said to Joe, "No way. That's really cool."

Tara shouted over the music. "What did he say?"

I repeated, "You have a four-year-old son?"

Immediately I felt a pain of betrayal like a knife going through my chest, and I shouted to Joe, "Wait a minute! Who told you that? We made a pact not to talk about our personal lives here with anyone!"

Joe quickly diffused my anger by explaining that Paul also has a five-year-old daughter. "Really?" It was like the whole world stopped for a second, and I had to let my brain catch up to this completely different scene.

*Paul's thoughts*

Yeah, Tara was really pissed at Chloe! Man, those beautiful eyes became daggers. I was thinking, "What's the big deal? I'm raising my daughter."

*Back to Tara*

We went from dancing the night away to immediately wanting to talk about our kids. We went hand and hand toward the beach, away from the loud music and crowd as we exchanged details of our real lives at home.

All of a sudden something shifted as if we knew each other all of our lives. Our hands clenched together tighter and tighter as I shared details of my struggles with my ex-husband and Paul shared his frustrations with his ex-wife. This emotional shift was fulfilling and exhilarating.

Paul shares, "I knew she was passionate because every time she talked about her ex, her hand grip got tighter."

It was the best walk. We talked and talked. Neither one of us were trying to prove anything or impress the other person. This was the beginning of us really connecting.

The warm breezy night turned into rain, and we ran for shelter. We ended up in Paul's room which he shared with Joe and Mike. It was very dark and quiet when we entered, so we figured we were alone. We held each other and began kissing passionately.

His hands were strong but gentle, and he touched me as if he knew me.

*Paul's perspective*

Oh my gosh, she was so hot! Perfect body, beautiful smile, great laugh, and wow, sexy!

Tara thought, *He made me feel beautiful, sexy, and at home all at the same time. Clothes were coming off, and the passion was heating up. I felt safe, yet wild with him.*

All of a sudden, we had a rude awakening that Mike, his friend, rolled over and was sleeping in the bed next to us. Oh no! How embarrassing! I never dressed so fast.

*Paul speaking*

I wanted to know where she was staying, I wanted her to stay the night. This can't be the last time I see her. I walked her to her room. She kissed me goodbye.

The next day, Tara, Chloe, and Melanie were on a plane headed back to Indiana.

At breakfast Joe asked, "How was your time with Tara? You guys disappeared after the she-has-a-son thing."

I responded "We had amazing sex in our room and finished up with Mike rolling over in the next bed." Mike swears that he didn't hear a thing… Yeah, right! We laughed our heads off.

# CHAPTER 2

# The Long-Distance Affair

As I am flying back home to Indiana, all I can think about is our amazing night together. We were not supposed to exchange numbers, but I discreetly gave Paul my business card. There was definitely something about this man that left a mark on me.

Paul lived in Western Massachusetts, and I lived in the Indianapolis area. We were both self-employed; Paul as an auto-mechanic, and I was a hair-stylist.

As I am getting back into the swing of regular life, my mind was still back in Cancun, Mexico. Talking about Paul with Chloe, she convinced me that it would be a great idea to send him a fax from our salon to Club Med with the statement, "Hey, if you haven't found anyone better, give me a call when you get back home!"

The next day, I received a dozen red roses with the card stating, "Haven't met anyone better!" This news excited everyone at the salon. It became the soap opera of the season.

*Paul speaking*

I really had no one to share this with. Joe and Mike agreed. "No phone numbers and no long-distance relationships." I had to keep this to myself. I stopped looking for girls for the rest of the vacation and just thought about Tara.

I lived with my sister at the time. Joe had cosigned on a house for me which helped me buy the duplex that I was living in. My sister, Kim, lived there with me and we were great roommates. I took care of her amazing dog Dakota, and she helped me with my daughter Kaeley.

When I came back from Cancun, she asked me, "How was it?"

I said, "F——ing perfect! I had a blast."

Kim asked, "Any souvenirs?" I knew that she meant girls.

I lied, "Nope not this time!"

*Back to Tara*

My son was on a vacation with his dad, so I was alone for a week after I returned from Club Med, therefore I was hanging out at Chloe's house. When I returned to my house, I had an answering machine full of messages! They were mostly from Paul. Driving home from the airport, he called me to stay awake, so he left these long messages of himself talking, joking, and even singing songs.

Paul explains, "I was stuck driving home from Boston in an ice storm in a customer's BMW that had a car phone. The drive home took hours, and I was still on cloud nine from my time with Tara."

Tara comments, "I was amused and amazed at his gift of gab. I called him! He was so easy to talk to! We stayed on the phone for hours until we set the date for him to fly out and visit me."

Furthermore, Paul states, "I wanted to know if this woman was for real. We have the same values, work ethics, ideas on how children should be raised, and we even had phone sex. Yeah, lots of it! I'm flying out there to see if she's for real, or if this is all a bunch of BS."

*Tara's thoughts*

I was thrilled to show him my real life! Life for me at the time was flowing smooth because I had an amazing career in one of the top salons in Indianapolis. I was living in a brand-new home in a beautiful, fast-growing town. I had a loving, protective family of friends around me. Most of all, my son was as cute as they come.

At this point in my life, I was not looking for a husband. I loved being single and free. For this reason, I decided to shock Paul to see what he was made of by cutting my hair super short without warning him. I also picked him up at the airport in a limousine just for a surprise.

Back then you could meet people at the gate of arrival. I was so nervous to see him again. Paul came up the rail and out of the doors and bam! Looking for the shock and awe on his face, I wrapped my arms around him and gave him a kiss. He smiled as he looked at me with adorning eyes and said, "Wow, it looks great!" He didn't even flinch! Test passed!

*Paul remembers*

We had talked on the phone almost every day since I got back from Mexico. We talked for hours, and our phone bills were horrendous. We had really become great friends, and I loved spending time with her even if it was just on the phone. But a visit? Yes!

Tara describes, "That first night was incredible! Dinner was a success, and I was so proud of my house that was built only six months prior to this time. I showed him around the house and pointed out all of the unfinished items and wallpaper borders I had planned to put up. We ended the night—or should I say, started the morning—with amazing sex."

About two hours of sleep was all I had before I had to get up for work on Saturday. I had a full day of hair clients from nine to three, so Paul came along for the ride in order to take the car for the day.

As a matter of fact, Paul states, "We hadn't talked about what I would do while she was at work. It hadn't even crossed my mind. I was still in a sex coma."

*Back to Tara*

I worked about twenty minutes from home but it was a straight shot on 116th street, from Fishers to Carmel, so he would have no trouble finding his way back home. Everyone at the hair salon was checking him out, especially the men! They oohed and aahed! Chloe couldn't wait to put him to the test to study him here on our territory.

Whew! Work was finished, and Paul was on time to pick m\
It was his turn to surprise me, because when I walked into my h\
after a tiring day of work, I was blown away! He fixed everything that
was unfinished and put up my wallpaper border in my bathroom! I
had imagined him sleeping all day because that's what I would have
done. He had me hooked at this very moment! What guy does this?

Paul's plan was: on the way home from dropping her off at
work, I stopped at Ace Hardware and bought the tools and supplies
that I needed to finish the "punch list" on her new home. I even did
the when-I-have-the-time-and-money wish list. I really liked her, and
I wanted to be the hero.

That night we went out to meet Chloe and friends for dinner.
Paul ordered two entrees because he wanted surf and turf and they
didn't offer it that way. He didn't seem to care what anybody thought
of him. We had a blast, and he was so easy to be with. Chloe greatly
approved!

*Paul's input*

If I pass the Chloe test, I'm in, but in for what? I have no idea.
I'm nine-hundred miles from home where I owned a successful business, and was raising my five-year-old daughter. I enjoyed driving my
corvette and a bitchin ski boat, so I had a very fulfilled, fun life! *What
am I doing?* But man, I really think there's something here!

The long-distance romance begins! He flew back to
Massachusetts, and I resumed life as I knew it.

Valentine's Day had approached, and I pondered what to send
Paul. What was appropriate for this new fling? As I searched the
stores, I came across a Dr. Seuss book called *Oh, the Places You'll Go!*
I knew it was the perfect gift—not too mushy, and not too predict-
able. I signed the front page with "Let's move mountains together!"
Because it is one of the statements in the story. Well, he loved it!

*I Knew It Was Too Good to Be True*

He sent me a great card with flowers. However, in the card, he had written me a three-page letter about his past.

Three pages of explaining to me that he had not one, not two, but three ex-wives and a daughter to go with each of them. He explained it to me like this.

"My first marriage happened while I was still a teenager because we got pregnant. My second marriage started off right but she controlled me to death. And my third marriage didn't work because she was out partying all the time."

As I was reading this letter describing each failed marriage, I started to feel sick to my stomach. How could this be? This is a recipe for disaster! He ended the letter with, "I wanted to be fair in letting you know about my past before moving forward. If you want to stop here, I understand."

*Paul's thoughts*

I had to tell her. I didn't have the balls to do it in person so I wrote it down. I had done some really stupid things in terms of relationships that had broken other hearts and mine as well.

I just couldn't spring this on her after one of us says those words. You know, the "Big 3"? No one had said it yet but the writing was on the wall. And the sex... Yeah, I'm giving her a way out.

*Back to Tara*

I gulped, but I didn't quite know how to swallow this. I let a few days pass while chewing on this news, but I respected the fact that he gave me the chance to bail out. My mind was saying, "Run!" But my heart said, he was worth the risk.

The long-distance phone calls were almost every night and about an hour long, and it was my turn to visit Massachusetts. The Boston airport was crowded and loud. I felt like a fish out of water until I saw Paul on the other side of the gate. Everything seemed so fast paced and hectic until we were on our way in the car, which ..... a silver, Volvo station wagon. He had prepared a picnic for the ride home with cheese, crackers, sliced meat, and wine. It was so romantic and unique.

We pulled up in front of a white cape in a quaint, New England neighborhood. Chicopee was the name of the town in the western part of the state. It was late at night so inside we went.

Paul lived with his sister, Kim, and his daughter, Kaeley, half of the week. Kim had a golden retriever named Dakota that also lived there. It was a two-family residence, so there was a single girl living on the other side of the house. The house was dark inside but homey. It was like going back in time for me and reminded me of Wisconsin where I grew up. There was a lot of snow on the ground and a snow-mobile parked in the front yard.

*Paul's input*

My sister, Kim, was away with her boyfriend, Pete, and Kaeley was at her mother's for the weekend.

I pulled out all the stops for this visit—picnic on the ride home, fire in the fireplace, more wine, candles. That weekend was a blast which included snowmobiling, driving out to the mountains, cooking some Portuguese dishes, and even leaving the room to pass wind! And then there was the *sex*! So why am I the only one still talking about how amazing the sex is?

Rollerblading was the new trend at that time and Paul loved to skate. He was very good at it because he played hockey in high school. We spent our time skating, and walking around the best new England artsy towns like Northampton and driving to the mountains. Of course we had lots of sex. In fact, Paul loved to cover the bed in soft red rose petals and have candles burning on the headboard shelf. He was a Portuguese, lover boy. He had me hooked!

# CHAPTER 3

# The Family Introductions

Paul and I were ready to introduce our children to one another. I will never forget Josh's look on his face when I introduced him to Paul. He was four years old with the brightest blue eyes and curly brown hair.

That cute little face turned into the best scowl he could muster when I said, "Josh, I want you to meet my friend, Paul!"

Well, Paul didn't let that scowl intimidate him. He scooped Josh up in his arms and without hesitation, said, "Come on, let's go for a ride on my skates!"

Paul skated off with him in his arms down the street of my neighborhood. By the time they returned, Josh had a huge smile on his face. They were instant buddies!

Paul adds, "Josh was a lot of fun. He was a real easy kid to fall in love with. As a child, he had lots of energy and hated going to bed. A lot like me, just hated to end the day."

Kaeley was five years old, and she was a little shy but very content and accepting. She had dirty-blond hair and the biggest brown eyes that lit up when she saw her daddy. We picked her up from kindergarten, and Paul introduced me while we were in the car. She didn't have any reaction, as if it was no big deal.

*Paul*

Unfortunately, Kaeley had seen a couple of women come and go in my life. When a relationship ended, we'd talk about it and just moved on and never really brought it up again.

Tara and I agreed that if our kids didn't get along, this was going to be a deal breaker. Up until this time, neither of us had said the "Big 3"—I love you. We both met each other's children on their own turf, but they hadn't met each other.

We decided to meet somewhere in the middle. Kaeley and I arrived to the hotel pretty late. It was a ten-hour drive for us from central Massachusetts, but we had a blast with lots of snacks, stories, and jokes. The biggest plus was that she was going to meet a new friend. They got along fabulous! Josh woke up when we got there, and they hugged, giggled, and fell asleep on the pull out.

"I was both relieved and terrified at the same time." I knew that if they didn't get along at least my life was going back to what it was, and it was a good life. Now they've met both of us, seen us together, met each other, and instantly bonded…

*Back to Tara*

Josh and I flew out to Massachusetts for another big test. The test was, Would Josh be happy or content at Paul's house?

He was so excited to fly to Boston to see Paul that he asked multiple people on the plane if they were going to visit Paul because he figured we were all going to the same place. Kaeley and Paul met us at the gate with balloons and big smiles. As soon as we were heading to Chicopee from Boston—about a two-hour ride—they were giggling in the backseat! It was an instantaneous friendship. Josh could make her laugh like nobody could.

Back and forth, we traveled for five more months. One day, while we were driving through Huntington (a beautiful, small hill town) to visit our favorite spots, Paul pulled the car over, along a rapidly flowing stream.

He turned to look at me intensely and said, "I need to tell you something." He paused and looked into my eyes. "I love you."

While blushing, I looked into his eyes and said, "I love you too."

This was the beginning to a whole new level of struggles and excitement! Who was going to drop their whole life and move?

I volunteered. New England made me feel alive and had such charm and variety. It reminded me a lot of my childhood in Wisconsin with the hills, rivers, and lakes. Not too long ago, I had just proclaimed after purchasing my new house, "It looks like I'm going to live here a long time!" Ha, ha, that's what happens when you make a declaration like that.

I need to back up to the most difficult introduction to make, which involved Paul and my parents. My mom was nice to everyone, but as soon as you left the house, she judged everything you said and did. My stepdad was totally intimidating because he was 6'4" tall and weighed 250 pounds.

He was so unapproachable and put an awkwardly tense feeling in the atmosphere. It always embarrassed me and so I would avoid bringing guests home as much as possible.

Paul was very self-confident as I made known, and when they met him, I could see that my parents were not impressed. They acted nice to his face, but I knew they were going to shred him to pieces after we left. Paul thought they were friendly, and couldn't understand why I felt so nervous.

Paul adds, "I don't recognize wolves in the woods. At the time, I just thought the best about everyone. Tara was nothing like her family. Nothing."

Paul's family was like a dream. I will never forget the day I met most of them. We all met at an amusement park called Riverside. Josh was with me, and he fit in perfectly with Paul's nephews and nieces. They were friendly and non-judgmental. Now remember, I am possibly to be Paul's fourth wife, so they had every right to act a little cautious. They welcomed us in as if we were the first.

# CHAPTER 4

## The Move

We have dated long distance for about five months, and we were going to go broke if we didn't take this relationship to the next level. Paul is a strong leader type, and as soon as I volunteered to move, he began to pick and plan for a moving date.

I was so in love that I didn't think twice about the sacrifices I would be making or the heartache it would cause my parents, ex-husband, his family, or my friends. It was full steam ahead!

Similarly, Paul's thoughts are we were definitely in the "love fog." And the sex was still amazing! We were determined to make it. We were convinced that we were really in love, and this time was going to be different.

July was the target! Breaking the news to my parents, my boss, and Josh's father was difficult. My parents were in shock and tried to convince me to wait a year.

My boss was surprised and challenged me with saying, "What about your cosmetology license?"

I replied, "Massachusetts has reciprocity with Indiana. Isn't that awesome?"

He said in a joking way, "Figures!"

Sam, Josh's dad, was very mature in his reaction. He didn't give me permission, but he said he would think about it. We had a marriage counselor that we both respected, so I called to make an appointment with her to receive professional advice. I had to promise Sam that I would not take Josh's whole childhood away from him.

When we met with the counselor, she advised that the child stay with me for the younger years because it is very important for the child to bond with the mother at a young age. When Sam heard this fact, he agreed to allow me to move Josh to Massachusetts. Whew!

The battle begins! I had no idea what was brewing behind the scenes. After everyone on my end realized that this was actually going to happen, their true colors came out. Colors that I didn't know existed especially from my mom.

What I was about to experience completely took me by surprise. She called me as Paul and I were busy running errands in Indiana, wrapping up loose ends for Josh and I to move.

She sternly said, "Tara, I need you to meet me at your divorce attorney's office right now because I have some information about Paul that you need to know."

I could feel her angst and thoughts of horrible things were running through my head as I replied, "You are at my attorney's office? What the f——! Okay… I guess I will meet you there!"

I looked at Paul with panic in my eyes and inquired, "Is there anything you need to tell me about your past that I don't know, because my mom seems very confident that she has something on you!"

Paul calmly and assuredly replied, "I have told you everything about my past, and there is nothing that I am hiding from you."

"Are you sure?"

"Yes, I'm sure!"

Tara peeled out of the driveway, and I was in a panic. What the f—— did I do? I called home to my parent's house in Massachusetts for some advice and moral support. To my surprise, my brother from California was there.

I told him what had just happened and he told me, "Run! Get the f—— out of there and get to the airport. I'll pay for the airline ticket. Call a cab and go! Dude, if this a sign of how her family is, you don't want any part of that sh——!"

*Tara speaking*

As I entered my attorney's office, I made eye contact with my mom and I was thinking to myself, "Who is this woman?" She didn't look like my mom.

I explosively asked, "What is this meeting all about?"

My mom proceeds to say, "I have reason to believe that Paul is a pedophile!"

I about choked as I yelled, "What?"

She replied as she gave it to the attorney, "I found this picture in the dresser drawer of your bedroom." It was a picture of Josh and Kaeley running naked up the stairs of Paul's house to get in the tub. I had taken the picture on one of my visits.

I turned and looked at her with disgust, and I chuckled, "This is your evidence? Wow! You are stretching for anything to keep me from moving! And you must have snuck into my house and snooped through my drawers to find this picture! Why didn't you come to me first if you really believe this to be true?"

She denied that she snooped in my house in front of the attorney. I asked the attorney if she had evidence to hinder us from moving Josh, she replied, "If they report that they have suspicion of abuse, it could delay your move." I left with my heart heavy, confused, outraged, and shocked that my mother could think so little of me.

The U-Haul trailer is packed up, and we are heading out the next day. Josh was spending his last day with his dad, and I needed to pick him up after dinner. Paul and I pull up in front of Sam's house and noticed that the whole family was there to say goodbye to Josh.

As I walk up the driveway, Sam came over to me and said, "Josh doesn't want to go with you, and I won't make him."

In all frustration, I replied, "We agreed on this. You signed the attorney's statement! Of course, he doesn't want to leave with all of your family not making it easy!"

Just then, Sam's father came closer down the driveway and yelled, "Why don't you think through your head instead of your c___ when it comes to what is best for your son?" Then all of the family joined with yelling obscenities which followed with Josh yelling, "I don't want to go to Massachusetts!"

Sam could tell that I was feeling totally ganged up on and noticed Paul was starting to get out of the car.

Sam interceded as he scolded, "Everybody shut up and stay out of this!"

He came over to me and said, "Look, I will bring him by your house in the morning, and if he wants to go with you, I will let him go."

Paul and I agreed to that, but we called the authorities as soon as we left, and they confirmed to us that we had legal right to take him. If Sam would not give him over to us, we could call them, and they would force him to hand him over.

The police were on standby the next morning.

The next morning, Sam came by with Josh. We walked him through the empty house for closure and finished packing the trailer. Josh expressed his desire to go with us, so Sam left.

It was a long, hot trip to Massachusetts as our air conditioner was broken, and I was so exhausted from all of the drama. Josh seemed happy and excited to see Kaeley and his new friends. We made it home just in time to go to New Hampshire for the yearly family reunion.

# CHAPTER 5

## Family Dynamics

As we drove into the parking lot of the Naswa Resort on Lake Winnipesaukee, loud cheering came from the beach as Paul's whole family came to greet us. Included in the gang were his four siblings, their spouses, and of course, his parents. Paul's nephews, who were twins, and his nieces all came up to especially greet Kaeley and to welcome Josh again. They all made Josh and myself feel loved and accepted. We all stayed in cabins on the beach front which included shared meals, playing card games, fishing tournaments, boating, and waterskiing. I had never experienced anything like it. There was not one argument the whole week! How is that possible? Maybe it was just Portuguese culture.

*Back to a little history of my family*

My family was so dysfunctional. I have a sister four years younger than me and a brother fourteen years younger. My mom remarried when I was in the sixth grade to a very tall, average looking man. He was funny and nice until he was our father. Then the switch happened, and he became intimidating and difficult to communicate with.

My mom also changed. It had been the three of us for twelve years. The dynamics especially changed when my parents found Jesus. They started to go to different churches and became foster parents to wild teenagers. All of this happened when I was thirteen, and it just stirred up the rebellion in me like a tornado.

We lived in Wisconsin at the time, and the final straw happened when I decided to run away with a neighbor boy. They sent me to live with my stepdad's sister and brother-in-law in Indiana. My uncle Dean and aunt Marie were the kindest people I had ever met. Uncle Dean especially made you feel like you were the only person in the room when he talked to you. He really had a way with youth. In fact, he was an English and drama teacher in a high school. He could relate to me and make me laugh at myself. Aunt Marie was kind, but she was more serious and seemed stressed at times. I loved living with them because they had a strict routine, and I always knew what was expected of me. I respected them.

Shortly after my sophomore year in high school, my parents moved to Indiana to the same neighborhood as my aunt and uncle. They placed us in private Christian school and found a neighborhood church. Complete reset!

However, it didn't change the rebelliousness inside of me. It stirred it up even more, but I just became a better liar. Even when my parents sent me to Bible College in Lakeland, Florida, I ended up suspended for drinking. After that, I ended up going to Cosmetology School and absolutely loved it.

# CHAPTER 6

# The Five-Year Glue

The routine of real life was setting in. Paul worked twelve-hour days, Monday through Saturday, and I needed to be home for Josh to transition as smoothly as possible to our new home. We frequently went for hikes, bike rides, and boating excursions with the kids on the weekends.

Our first summer together was still very hot, sexually. I loved to think of ways to shock Paul. For instance, I walked into his shop with an overcoat on and nothing else, flashed him in his office, and then left him with a smile on his face. I would also leave signs on the front door of our house with instructions to take a shower and come naked to a romantic candlelit dinner. This only happened of course when the kids were with their other parents.

Later in the fall, I realized that I was late with my period. I will never forget seeing the positive results on the stick. Even though, the timing was off, we were completely delighted with the news. By that December, we eloped on a cruise ship to the Bahamas.

*Paul's comment*

We had so many failed relationships between us that we were too embarrassed to have a wedding. Tara's mom had meddled too far in our relationship so I told her in a phone call screaming match, that she had better stay out of our lives.

After the love cloud lifted, Paul's temper became apparent, and I realized how much I was walking on egg shells. He worked long hours, stayed up late every night, and up early every morning. I wasn't working because I needed to be available for Josh. I hated feeling vulnerable so I would count loose change around the house to buy things for myself. Depending on a man was not easy for me.

The reality of dealing with ex-wives and husbands was no picnic but we tried the best we could to keep the peace. It was back and forth airplane trips to Indiana for Josh to see his dad, which was always heart wrenching for him. Kaeley's mom lived in the area, so she was bounced back and forth several times weekly.

On July 8, 1995, Rachel was born. The kids were excited to welcome her into our family. I can remember staring at her with amazement and thinking how perfect she was. I was overwhelmed with joy! She arrived exactly on her due date, and the labor and delivery went so quick and easy. I had her on a Saturday and Paul went back to work on the very next Monday. We brought her to New Hampshire for the family reunion which was two weeks later. She was an easy baby all the way around!

We loved camping! And Paul loved the Connecticut river! The boat was our life in the Summer. It was Paul's baby. He had a super cool, flat-bottom speed boat that skimmed on top of the water so fast that it felt like we were flying.

He loved to waterski, barefoot ski, and teach waterskiing. There was a waterski show team on the river called the Oxbow Water Ski Show Team, and we joined it that summer after Rachel was born. It became our life and religion in the summers.

We had three family groups in our lives that we called our life. The waterski club, Paul's Auto and Marine staff, and our Catholic Church friends. The Oxbow Waterski show team was a club that put together a ski show with many different acts; from pyramids to ski jumping to ballet line to barefoot skiing.

Along with these acts were skits, dances, and comedy. An emcee tells the story, introduces the skiers, and explains the acts. It was similar to circus life. We camped at the site on the weekends which involved crazy partying!

We made costumes, props, and practiced our routines all day. It was a very different life, but our whole family loved it.

Paul explains, "I always loved the water, boats, and skiing. It's all I ever wanted to do. As a kid when we were on vacation, I used to look at wooden boats with my dad and dream that one day, I'd have my own antique boat. Pretty much my whole adult life, owning a boat almost eclipsed owning a car. Any spare moment I can get to the water, I would."

Paul's Auto and Marine was our business in Chicopee, Massachusetts. It was a neighborhood garage off of a main street in Chicopee. The location was perfect! The staff included a secretary, and two mechanics besides Paul.

We were best friends with the secretary and her family, which consisted of her husband and two boys. They were the same age as Josh and Kaeley. We spent almost every weekend with them camping, hanging out at one of our homes with lots of drinking when we were not at the Ski club.

Our Catholic friends were Danny and Lynn, and they had two daughters who were older than our kids. We often went to their home for amazing home-cooked meals! We had a blast with them and would usually see them at church and church activities which was almost always followed with drinks and great life stories at their house.

Within those years, we met a few milestones in life. For example, we purchased a garage for Paul's business. I started a new part time job at a hair salon. During all of this period, Kaeley's mom and I started to become friends by working out together at the gym after taking the kids to school. All of these milestones were working together for a perfect storm.

*Paul's input*

Yeah, so this is a little weird. My wife and ex-wife are workout exercise buddies. Tara asked me first if it was okay.

I said, "As long as I am never the topic of conversation..." Not so sure they stuck to that rule.

*Tara*

Our daughter, Rachel, was the glue that was holding us together in this time period. I was always feeling insecure of what Paul was feeling about me, and he was extremely controlling. He had wandering eyes whenever we passed by a good-looking girl, and I would catch him making eyes with them. He was always the life of the party and would hug other girls way too long. Women loved him because he was funny and caring.

I started to get weird feelings in my stomach about his relationship with his secretary. They had a thriving friendship, and we spent almost every weekend at her house which involved a lot of drinking! I always talked myself out of feeling jealous because she was not a beauty queen by any means. She was tomboyish and a little heavy. She did have a great personality and was an excellent help to Paul in the shop. She also seemed happily married.

One day, before we purchased the new shop, I spontaneously came to visit Paul at the old shop. I looked through the garage door window, and I thought I saw them kissing next to one of the cars in the garage.

I thought I was hallucinating because I couldn't decide if it really happened or if I imagined it.

I went in to the garage and after I spent some time there, I was walking out, and Paul asked me if everything was okay.

I responded, "Yeah, why?"

"Just checking." He sighed and shrugged his shoulders.

After this day, I started to spiral downward with haunting thoughts that drove me to start drinking by 4:00 p.m. just to take the edge off. We camped with them, and I always had my eyes on their interactions with each other. It was in the air, but I couldn't put a finger on it.

*Paul's defense*

After Rachel was born, Tara was always mad at me. She'd have that look every day when I came home from work, like she was pissed off at me. She accused me of lots of sexual things, even with guys, and they were not true. Yeah, I had a roaming eye. So what? Don't we all?

The other dynamic was Paul's controlling actions. As I became more independent with my job and making new friends, his behavior became more possessive. My boss was an attractive Greek woman, and as we were all out dancing one night, she blurted out, "Boy, your husband is a flirt!" That truth went through me like a knife.

These were the signs that haunted me. I had no one to talk to about my suspicions, so I started secretly trying to find a counselor. This venture was frustrating in itself. All that I had for reference was the yellow pages. The first counselor was downtown Springfield where I had to parallel park my Jeep Grand Wagoneer. That was enough to rattle my nerves alone. The building was plain, cold, and dark as I walked up the stairs to find the office. The woman was expressionless and unappealing as she called me in to her office.

When she asked me why I had come to see her, I began to rattle on as much information as possible. Trying to get to the point as quickly as possible so she could give me the desperately sought-after advice. It felt like I was talking to a wall. Of course, she wasn't going to tell me what to do, and she couldn't tell me Paul was a monster, so I left feeling like I just swam in vomit.

It was New Year's Eve, and Paul decided to have our Paul's Auto and Marine Christmas/New Year's Eve celebration by renting a limousine and going bar hopping in the city. This was when I couldn't ignore the flirtatious eyes of Paul's secretary any longer. With alcohol involved it was more evident. I felt myself getting filled with rage, but I kept shoving it down with drinks. I will never forget the next day hangover from that party. I thought I was dying and it lasted two whole days and nights.

That was it. I confronted Paul, "Are you in love with Debbie?" And he just laughed.

"She is just my really good friend."

Feeling so frustrated, I begged him to see a counselor with me.

He confidently said, "Okay… I will!" Just to prove that he was innocent.

The counselor he found was a woman recommended to us by a friend from the ski club. The office was in a large building with huge windows and updated décor. The counselor found us in the waiting area and introduced herself. She was personable and seemed to be professional.

*Aaaah*, I thought inside my head, "There is hope that she will hear me."

"Tell me a little about yourselves," she opened with.

As soon as Paul told her he was an auto mechanic, she interrupted him with questions about her Volvo issues. I sat there with amazement that Paul was going to charm her with answers to her problems.

Finally, she came back to us and looked upon me with, "So… why are you here to see me?"

I again spewed out as much information as possible as fast as possible to paint a picture of what I was experiencing.

She turned to Paul with no emotion and asked, "Are you having an affair?"

He plainly stated, "No!" That seemed good enough for her, and she looked back at me as if to say, "So there's your answer."

We walked out of there with more tension than we came. We continued to see her a few more times until I was convinced that we were getting nowhere. After all this frustration, I decided in my mind that I was going to live in denial about our relationship, and let the chips fall where they may.

# CHAPTER 7

# The Chips Fell

There is always a calm before the storm. Paul and I were very involved in the Water ski Show Team, and our team won the regional competition. The whole team wanted to travel to Ohio to compete in the national Show Ski competition. We decided to join the adventure. We were serious and practiced as much as possible, and this was keeping my mind off my reality.

Out of forty teams, we came in tenth place. It was being televised by ESPN, and we felt like we were on top of the world. Another plus, my parents were there because we were three hours from Indianapolis. They drove to see the show and to watch Rachel for us. Here was my chance to rub it in their face that we were a happy, successful family unit.

The fall of that year, the ski club put on an amazing haunted hay ride as a fund raiser. This was right up my alley for fun. I loved Halloween, and I loved to dress in costume! Paul and I were always all in with these activities which kept us focused on others things other than our relationship. Big blow ups would happen in the midst of them, but we kept sweeping them under the rug.

After the summer season, we went right into activities such as church events, school events, and sports events. Paul is extremely social, and I enjoyed all of these activities especially with alcohol. I started to notice that we were including it in our coffee at the soccer games, church picnics, and almost daily in our evenings. It was our tranquilizer.

I can remember saying to Paul, "If I ever had to quit drinking..."

*Back to my dad's call*

This brings us back to the time that I received the call from my dad. It was pretty ironic because my sister and I had communicated on the phone that it would be so cool to find our dad. I remember her desire with doubt in her tone. "But where would we ever start?"

The name Smith (his last name) was innumerable! So when I heard my dad's voice on the other end of the phone, I was shocked at the timing!

It is funny how things begin to happen when you surrender the fight and let go. My dad invited me to the Smith family reunion, and from this point forward, life was never going to be the same. I thought to myself, *Now I will know what is missing!*

Suddenly, Paul and I had a whole new focus which helped me to stay in denial of our problems. That summer in July, as we were flying to Madison, Wisconsin, my mind was racing with thoughts like, "What was I going to say?" Or "How were we going to get along?"

Paul and I were getting along pretty well because of the adventure and the possible inheritance coming our way. Our plane landed, and we rented a car to drive another two hours of back-country highways to reach the park.

We finally get settled in our hotel room and make arrangements to meet my dad for dinner.

*Paul's perspective.* I was totally for this! I had two daughters that I was estranged from. I thought, *Wow, how cool for Tara to meet her dad after all these years.* I had asked many times about him, and she often said that in some ways, I reminded her of him.

It was like watching water boil waiting for the clock to strike 6:00 p.m. Paul had his normal bathroom call and asked me to find him something to read. I glanced around the room and found nothing until I opened the desk drawer and found a Bible. "There is nothing except a Bible!" I loudly chuckled.

He quickly responded, "No thanks!" But then he quickly rethought it and yelled, "Wait! I'll take it!"

"Here ya go!" With my shoulders shrugged, I handed it to him.

He came out quoting a scripture that he read, "Don't judge anyone lest you be judged! By the measure you judge, you also will be judged."

"Hmmm…" we both said.

The knock at the door took my breath away! Here it is. The moment I've been waiting for since I was a young girl. I felt so insecure, excited, and scared all at the same time. I opened the door, and there he stood, probably just as insecure and scared as I was. He had a plaid dress shirt on and jeans. He was bald and had a moustache framing his goofy smile with missing teeth. He was not the handsome, tall, dark-haired native American that I pictured in my mind.

His wife followed him in the room with Dolly Parton big hair and the body of a teenager. Tyler, their son, also came with them, and he was a gentle, nice-looking young man. They were so sweet in their character and mannerisms. My dad gave me a necklace, which was an Indian character which represented protection.

After the ice had broken a bit, we went to Outback Steakhouse, and my dad and I both ordered the rib eye steak. I noticed we both held our hands in our lap the same way. I also noticed how soft he talked and realized how much we are alike. His wife was sweet as can be and called my dad Lovey. She honored him and looked out for him. Tyler resembled me a bit and was the nicest brother I could want. The first meeting went well, and I felt relaxed!

*Paul's input*

Tara's dad was really nice but superhard to hear—so much like Tara. He talked about his life, where he lived, his two other children, Tyler and Violet, and stepdaughter Brenda. He was from Antigo, Wisconsin, but currently lived in Flagstaff, Arizona. He explained a little about each of his siblings and some of their spouses.

He especially warned us to watch out and stay clear of his brother, Don. "He's a Jesus-freak, Bible-thumper."

I remember thinking, "No problem. I'm good staying clear of him."

Tara and I laughed and said, "Thanks for the warning."

*Tara*

The next meeting was breakfast! Another nervous encounter with meeting more of my aunts and uncles that I heard of but did not remember. (Keep in mind, I haven't seen my father or his family in thirty years, since I was four years old.) When Paul and I walked into the restaurant, we were brought to an event room with a huge table filled with my newfound relatives.

My dad quickly stood up to introduce me to his brothers and sisters. I could feel my face getting more blush as each one was greeting me. Last but not least, I meet my Uncle Don, who is one of his youngest brothers.

Uncle Don stood up and reached his hand out to me as he boldly asked me, "Hi, I'm Uncle Don… Do you know Jesus?"

I felt my face turn on fire! I stuttered, "Um, yes, I guess so."

And he looked me right in the eyes as he still had my hand in his and asked, "Do you put Him first in your life?"—paused—"Before your husband and your kids?"

Now I was tripping over my tongue and didn't know how to respond as I stuttered even worse with "Um…um, I… I…don't know." While shaking my head and shrugging my shoulders as I sat down.

I quickly shuffled through my purse looking for my cigarettes. I wanted to run and hide at this moment but was trapped and worse yet, I had to sit next to him.

Trying to hide in my menu didn't keep my uncle Don from pursuing me in conversation. He lit up a cigarette and proceeded to draw me in with his experience with Jesus. I was so relieved that he smoked so I could light up a cigarette to calm my nerves. It also made my guard come down a little.

I put down the menu and engaged with him one on one. He had a big, teddy-bear presence and wholeheartedly loved Jesus.

He went on to say, "Peanut… I was completely in the gutter of life. I had lost everything and had nothing to my name when I called out to Jesus. He pulled me out of the pit, and I felt his love for real. I heard his voice and felt his presence. He has given me my trucking business and put me back on my feet."

Uncle Don's face lit up when he talked about God, and I could see a joy for life in him that was intriguing.

He told lots of jokes and funny stories. He would kick his baseball cap back so that his ears would stick way out and fold the brim straight up. Hilarious. He also had these piercing blue eyes. Deep.

After breakfast, we all headed to the park where the reunion was taking place. I kept my ears open, waiting to hear something about the inheritance my dad told me about, but nobody was speaking of any such thing. Everyone was setting up tables and food but pretty much keeping to their own groups. I found myself looking for Uncle Don and wanting to be around him. He had such a unique sense of humor and was a great storyteller of all the crazy things the Smith's did as children.

They were extremely poor farmers.

They would play with bows and arrows and he claimed, "Out of eleven kids, which would be twenty-two eyes, we only lost one eye!"

He also told stories of how they would do crazy stunts with their animals. For instance, bringing a pony into their house while their parents were gone. They continued to be wild, as they grew older and caused all kinds of trouble. So much so that the town of Antigo would not allow more than two Smith's to be in the same bar at once or any public place. Hence, my dad changed his last name to Bickford.

The weekend quickly came to an end, and we flew back to New Hampshire in time for Paul's family reunion. Paul and I had drinks on the plane to celebrate the adventure we had and arrived to his reunion pretty buzzed. I knew somehow that I was never going to be the same.

*Now at the end of that summer, the shit hit the fan!*

Life was getting back to normal as it does every year at the end of August. I had been busy with cutting hair as usual before school starts. One particular Saturday morning, I had an appointment with Debbie's husband to cut his hair.

He and I did not have much in common so conversation was not easy. He was as quiet as I was.

He plopped down in my hair chair at my in-home salon, took off his baseball cap, and said, "Do your magic!"

He was a simple guy, rugged type who liked to drink, smoked lots of pot on the weekends, and played sports with his kids.

As I am clipping away, randomly he asks, "Does it bother you that Paul bought Debbie flowers for her birthday?"

All of a sudden, everything that I had been pushing down inside started to come up, and I could feel my knees start to shake.

"Yes, does it ever!" I responded, as I stopped cutting his hair for a moment and looked him in the eyes through the mirror.

"Do you get the same yucky feeling in your gut about their friendship as I do?" I asked.

He went on to say, "Oh yes, for a while now. I always wanted to ask you about it but didn't know how to bring it up. As a matter of fact, I have something I need to tell you and show you."

All of my insides now were tensing up, and I was scared and relieved at the same time because this means I wasn't paranoid after all. But this information could change my whole life.

"I have proof that something has been going on. I found a letter in our bureau last weekend from Debbie to Paul." He explained, "I wasn't sure if you were ready to see it so I left it at home, but I will go home and bring it here for you to read."

"I knew it! But I could never put my finger on it! Please let me see it!" I pleaded. I threw off his cape and dusted him off and away he went. I was biting my nails to the quick and pacing my house as I waited for him to return with the letter.

I felt like my blood was boiling! Mark, Debbie's husband, pulled up to the front of my house and came back in to show me the letter.

As I began to read it, all of the *aha's* in my head were going off.

"I knew it! I knew it! I knew it!" There was a sentence that said, "I love you more than my own kids."

That sentence threw me into a rage inside. I suddenly felt so sorry for Mark. This was his wife!

The other sentence that royally pissed me off was "I will always love you, and maybe in the future, we will end up together."

My thought was, *Let me make that happen for you sooner than later!*

I took a breath and looked at Mark and inquired, "What should we do about this?"

He replied, "Let's get them off guard and confront them."

I agreed with him, saying, "I will find a babysitter for my kids tonight, and I will tell Paul to invite you guys over for dinner."

He said, "Great idea!" It was a plan!

I called the daughter of our friends, Lynn and Danny, and asked for an emergency favor to pick up our kids for the night. Her name was Nicole, and she and her sister often babysat and loved our kids.

She asked, "Is everything okay?"

I replied, "Yes, but I need to have an important conversation with some friends, and it is not for little ears to hear." She agreed to help.

It was a sunny evening, and the grass was getting brown on our front lawn from the dry end of summer. Mark and Debbie arrived. Paul and I came out to meet them in the yard. We started with smiles, small talk about the day, and smoking our cigarettes. Mark and I made eye contact with a subtle nod of the head.

I interrupted our small talk with, "The real reason we are here right now is to talk about the affair you are having with each other."

It was like somebody hit the pause button on the universe.

Paul defensively replied, "What are you talking about?"

Mark responded, "Well, I found a letter addressed to you in my wife's bureau from home declaring her love for you!"

Suddenly, the rage burning inside of me came bursting out with rage in my eyes toward Paul. "I knew it. How could you lie to my face over and over again!" And I turned to glare at Debbie and said, "And you!" I screamed, "How could you live with yourself as you pretend to be my friend and babysit for my kids!"

They both denied any action to their feelings.

Paul's thought was, *How can you blame me for a letter found in her drawer?*

"I didn't write it!"

I couldn't believe their denial! Feeling so frustrated, I started losing my cool as I began hurling F-bombs at them so loud that the neighbors could hear.

Paul had the nerve to try to quiet me down. "Tara, stop yelling! The neighbors…"

I yelled louder. "What? Are you embarrassed? Well, I don't care who hears about you've done!"

Debbie tried to put the whole blame on herself. She claimed, "It was a letter I wrote to Paul but never gave to him. He is in love with you, so please…don't leave him!"

Paul looked at Debbie and said, "You're fired! And I want all of your belongings out of the office by Monday."

And then he looked at Mark and said, "Mark, I'm so sorry."

Then Paul walked away toward the house with his head hanging down.

*Paul*

My thought was, "Are you kidding me?" Here we go, another divorce. We had a short-term physical fling about six months ago, and I cut it off. I couldn't take the guilt. We both agreed to take it to our grave and that would be the end of that. We had an emotional bond that grew over years of spending every day together. She would stand beside me at any city meetings, inspections, or public or legal things that I needed for work. I screwed this up! I saw it coming, and I did nothing to stop it. Tara looked at me with disapproval and distrust well before any of this happened, and now she had a reason. "Shit!" Denial—that's the answer.

*Tara*

Hatred was all I felt toward Paul and Debbie. It was like a volcano of emotion that kept spewing up and pain of betrayal was like the ashes smoldering in my heart.

"Where do I go from here?" Was my aching thought.

As I looked for possibilities in my mind, such as moving back to Indiana, I could hear my parents, friends, and ex-husband saying, with their heads shaking, "Told ya so!"

When I thought about staying in Massachusetts, I pictured constant torment and reminders of the betrayal. There was absolutely no way of staying in the marriage which left me no hope in any direction.

*Paul*

I have no idea what's coming next. These thoughts run through my head, *Is Mark going to pummel me? Am I going to come home to an empty home? Kids gone? Bank account empty? What about the business?*

Debbie helped me grow it from a small shop to a big repair center. I don't know the books, paperwork, the bank balances... "Shit, shit, shit, shit!" F—— it. I survived this three times before. I'll survive it again. Or maybe I'll just eat a bullet. Can I even do all this 'Start over again?' I was so ashamed of myself, my life, and my actions. What about our friends? She's so mad, she wouldn't even talk to me. I blamed it all on Debbie, saying that she wrote the letter not me. But Tara was not buying it. A lie is a lie.

A woman can smell a lie a mile away—especially Tara.

# CHAPTER 8

# The Rescue

I was trapped. I had no money of my own, no job, and no family. Kaeley's mom, Lana, and I had become pretty good friends because we had been working out together, and I had become her hairstylist. She was the only one I could confide in about the affair. Lana was attractive and very friendly. At times, I was jealous of her talented singing voice. She had a karaoke business that was quite successful, and Paul and I would visit the bars once in a while to support her.

Never would I sing even when she would try to convince me to join in. She and Paul were as amicable as possible. We always celebrated Kaeley's birthday and special events as one big family for Kaeley's sake.

Anyway, Lana invited me and Rachel to go to the beach with her and Kaeley for the weekend so that I could be away from Paul and think.

*Paul's thought*

Oh no! This is going to turn out bad. But what could I say? Tara held all the cards at this point. I was not in a position to make any demands whatsoever.

*Tara*

I jumped at the chance to get away! We went to New Hampshire and stayed on the boardwalk of Hampton beach in a cute little motel. It was so great to have an ocean atmosphere, have drinks with a girl friend, and play with the kids. Of course, Lana and I started to talk about Paul and the situation.

Lana right away stated, "I never liked that girl! I knew something was off!"

Then the flood gates flew open, and she vomited all of her woes with Paul and their marriage. Now I was even more furious inside about him, and the hate was overwhelming. When I returned from that weekend getaway, I was determined to leave him. I knew the direction to take, but how?

I came up with a solution. "Paul, I am writing up a contract that you will have to agree upon in order for me to stay even another day!"

I declared, "This is how it's going to be for the next year. I'm going to get a job and any money that I make or comes in for child support will be put into a savings account for me. I will be able to go on a girl's only vacation whenever I want. After one year, if things are miserable, I will take Rachel and all of the money in my savings to move out on my own."

I stated with confidence, "You must sign it!"

He agreed.

*Paul*

This was a really bad business/marriage deal, but I have no choice. Denial, right? This would put me on the ropes daily, performing as a husband.

It was way better than another divorce. This was a second chance, even with all the stipulations. It's better than no chance.

Back to work I go. Debbie was gone, and her desk was empty. The pictures of her family and special life events, all gone.

I have been in business in this city for over ten years. I have a huge customer base and a really full repair schedule of cars, boats, and trucks. Now no secretary to help with the paperwork.

I was the guy who dealt with the customers, diagnosed all the issues, and came up with the repair plan.

When I went to the bank to get things reconciled and see where we were financially, the business was 7k in the hole.

What? How could that be? We were making lots of money. Tara was going to kill me. She hated my business before all this happened. What was I going to do?

Meanwhile, our dear friend Lynn came to meet me at my shop. Tara had confided in her what was going on. We loved Lynn and Danny, and they loved us. They were not much older than us but they often were like big brother and sister to us.

Lynn asked if it was true about the affair. I denied it. She told me that if our marriage was going to work, I had to be totally in! "If you give it your all, it will work."

*Tara*

I found myself smoking more than a pack a day, and drinking every day. About one week had gone by since the signing of the contract, and I had been scraping wallpaper from our small dining room to turn into a hair salon. As I was scraping harder and harder, the thoughts of Paul and Debbie were tormenting me.

The imaginations that ran through my mind had me feeling so humiliated and betrayed, and it felt like a knife was jabbing me in the heart over and over again. I couldn't breathe, and I had to run out the house, and when I did, I couldn't stop running.

I ran and ran until I came to a huge oak tree that stood in our neighborhood cemetery. I loved this cemetery because it was a perfect place to walk or ride a bike without dogs attacking or cars hitting you. I used to walk and talk to God in this place.

Anyway, here I was, standing up against a tree, trying to catch my breath, and wailing like a baby. The pain was unbearable still, and all I could do was look up. And I started to put all my pain on God.

I screamed, "How can I live like this! Marriage sucks! You invented it! It doesn't work! What were you thinking? There's got to be more to life than this! How am I supposed to live with this?"

Exhausted from all of the screaming and crying, I closed my eyes and shut my mouth as I just listened to the quiet.

All that I could hear was, "Do you know Jesus?" followed by a moment of silence.

"Do you put him first in your life before your husband and your kids?"

I looked up and spoke out loud, saying, "Is that my answer? Are those two questions my answer?"

As I pondered those questions for the first time, I came up with the real answer which were, "No, I don't know You, Jesus," and "No, I don't put You first in my life."

Before I could really understand what that was going to look like, I cried, "I surrender, Jesus. I want to know You. Not just know about You but really know you, and I will put you first in my life! I can't do this on my own!"

Right after I spoke those words, I felt a warm sensation enter my heart. It was like hope became tangible. I could breathe better, and I could see a way out of this total wreckage. I began to walk back home, and I felt as if my head was lighter. Was this what hope felt like? Not sure at this point.

Later that day, our phone rang, and I answered, "Hello?"

"Hello, is this Peanut?"

"Yes, it is."

"Peanut! This is Uncle Don. Remember me?"

"Yes, of course!"

Uncle Don said, "You have been on my mind constantly. So I thought, I better call you! What's going on with you?"

I felt my throat tighten, and my mouth quivered while trying not to cry, "Well, I have been going through a crisis in my marriage, and I just surrendered my life to Jesus!"

"Well, it's no wonder you've been on my mind!" he excitedly proclaimed.

He asked, "Now, Peanut, does this crisis involve another woman?"

"Yes!" I replied. He went on to encourage and instructed me. "Forgive all involved!"

I did not hesitate to say, "Okay, I will."

Something inside of me knew that this was happening because of what happened in the cemetery earlier. I was ready to follow whatever my uncle Don was about to tell me. Ground zero is the picture of where my life was, and I was ready to leave my own opinions and hurts aside.

"How is Paul doing?" And he added, "Have you told him about surrendering to Jesus?"

"No, I haven't told him. We don't talk much," I explained.

"Oh," he paused, "Peanut, don't tell him about you and Jesus. Just love him. What I mean is, don't preach to him or praise the Lord in front of him. Wait until he leaves the house, then praise the Lord all you want. Now put him on the phone, I would like to say hi to him!" He chuckled.

Paul and Uncle Don chatted with small talk, had a few laughs, and then hung up.

The next day, I woke up with an amazing peace inside. Paul was off to work, and the kids were at school, so I had the house to myself. I found myself lying face down on my bed with my arms stretched out wide so that I could feel my heart being massaged by the Lord's hands. Something supernatural was happening to me, and I didn't care how strange it seemed. I just didn't want it to stop.

I jumped off the bed and ran down stairs and started to express what I was feeling out loud, "Wow! You are *real*, Jesus! You really are *real*! Oh my gosh! I can feel you massaging my broken heart! I can feel your peace all over me! You are *real*!" I shouted as I danced around the living room.

"I love you, I love you, I love you!" I was bursting with emotion. I felt like I was going to explode with joy.

"Thank you, thank you, thank you!" I cried with all of my heart. I found myself searching for a Bible because I wanted to know Jesus and read for myself what he is all about. I didn't have to look far because I surprisingly found one on our bedroom shelf. It was a paperback Bible that I don't ever remember seeing before.

I thought to myself, *Hmm, I wonder if I look up a word in the back, would it give me a page number to find that topic?*

I looked up marriage to see what Jesus has to say about it. There it was *marriage* with a couple of page numbers beside it. Thinking to myself, *That was too easy.* I looked at the passages and discovered that God hates divorce. This was so awesome to me because now I had some guidance without having to find a counselor.

*Paul's experience*

So it's about two weeks since it all hit the fan. It's time for our counseling appointment, and I came home from work to pick up Tara. Remember, marriage counseling is a stipulation of the contract that I had to sign.

She tells me, "I'm going to let the word of God be my counselor."

"What? Are you kidding me right now? I just took time off to come and pick you up for counseling, and you're not going? You have lost your f——in mind!"

To which, she replied, "I think you should go anyway without me."

This called for a total peel out in front of my house and a fifteen-minute angry drive to the counselor's office.

"How's it going and where's your wife?" he asked.

"Well, sir, I don't really know how to tell you this, but she said that she is going to let the word of God be her counselor, so she's not coming anymore."

He calmly replied, "I understand. I don't see huge success in that, but it does work for some." We talked for a while, and I went back to work.

*Back to Tara*

In the privacy of my own home, I am able to hear from God about marriage. I looked up wife next. I was shocked at what I read, but I knew deep inside that I was receiving wisdom from God. I read 1 Peter 3:1–4 which reads,

> And now let me speak to the wives. Be devoted to your own husbands, so that even if some of them do not obey the Word of God, your kind conduct may win them over without you saying a thing. For when they observe your pure, godly life before God, it will impact them deeply. Let your true beauty come from your inner personal-

ity, not a focus on the external. For lasting beauty comes from a gentle and peaceful spirit, which is precious in God's sight and is much more important than the outward adornment of elaborate hair, jewelry, and fine clothes. (The Passage Translation)

I thought to myself, *Whoa! That is old fashioned! Are you sure about that God? Hmm...well, I certainly have never been that kind of wife.*

After reading this over and over and also reading other Scriptures for wives, I realized the hate I felt for Paul was turned to hope. I made a deal with God.

"Okay, God. I can see that I've never followed your blueprints for wives in marriage. I will tear up the contract I made Paul sign, and I will try it your way, like a recipe! This is my last shot, so this marriage is in your hands!"

I had vision! I had instruction! I had peace of mind to move ahead in life. It didn't take long before I had the opportunity to test God's recipe for marriage.

Paul asked me, "Hey, the guys from the ski club invited us to a cookout party at the park on the river. The kids are invited. Do you want to go?"

I replied, "Sure, whatever you think."

He hesitated and then asked, "Well...yes, but I want to know what you think!"

I said, "I think it's up to you!"

Hmm...this felt very different because I was giving him the reins on the decision even though I didn't think it would be the best place for our kids to be. We packed up the kids and spent the day with our partying friends, except I didn't drink or get high with them. I was completely content to play with the kids and chat with the girls. As we were leaving, the police showed up, but we had no worries because I was driving. Paul was starting to see and feel the peace of mind I had.

*Paul's point of view*

Okay. Wait, wait, *wait* just a minute! Felt different? How about you rarely trusted to just leave things up to me. You usually had something negative to say or something to add. And inside I'm saying to myself, "Oh crap! Just shup up and say yes so we can get moving."

My thought was, *Well, it doesn't really matter because I'm going with or without you.* But that was all precontract, and Lynn said, "Put your all toward this marriage." "Whatever you think?" I felt a ton of weight fall on my shoulders.

All of a sudden, I was responsible for this family, where we go and what we do and how.

We went to the lake for a pig roast/keg party. We used to hang out with families that partied while their kids played together. Drinking and smoking pot went well that night, but I didn't dare tell my buddies what was going on with Tara and me. All I know is that I was getting pretty wasted.

When it came time to leave, Tara asked, "Would you like me to drive?"

I knew she didn't drink much at all that night.

Usually I would say, "No, I got this," and drive home drunk, stoned or both with my family in the car. But this time, it was different. I felt like I could really trust her. She asked me and didn't tell me. This was so different.

I gave her the keys and said, "Sure, why not." Just as we were backing out of our parking spot, the police pulled in to bust up the party. I would have gotten a DUI for sure. I thought to myself, *Hmmm, what's going on here?*

# CHAPTER 9

# Miracles

A couple of weeks have gone by, and almost every day, I would call my uncle Don. He was praying for me and helping me off the ledge now and then.

I would call him and say things like, "I can't do this! He is so self-righteous!"

Uncle Don would always encourage me to be patient and wait on the Lord. Eventually, Paul approached me and said, "You seem so different lately! Are you on something? If so, I want some!"

Then I expressed to him as matter of fact, "I want to serve the Lord with my life."

Condescendingly, he put his arm around me and started to pat my back while saying, "I am so happy for you!"

I wanted to turn my head so that I could stick my finger down my throat and barf! He proceeded to sit down on our outdoor porch swing, and he looked down as he said, "I have done too many bad things to serve the Lord. It's too late for me!"

"It's never too late," I replied.

Uncle Don listened to me explain all of this and said, "Peanut, we need to fast and pray for him!"

I replied, "What's fasting?"

He explained, "We don't eat for three days while we pray and read the Bible to fill us up."

"What? How can you not eat for three days without dying?"

Uncle Don chuckled and replied, "God is nourishing you as you trust him by praying, and we eat the living bread [Word of God] to feed our spirit."

"Okay..." I said, reluctantly. "I will try it."

For the next three days, I skipped all my meals, drank a lot of coffee, and read the Bible when I felt hungry. We prayed together every day, and I began to see crazy coincidences happen. For instance, we would sit down to watch a movie, and it would happen to be about a pastor who ran from God. Or Paul would come home from work and give me a Christian CD and some booklets that he picked up at a Christian store and said, "Here... I thought you might enjoy these."

The most powerful sign I saw was at the end of fasting. We were in the kitchen, and I was sitting at the table. Paul was standing behind the island, preparing some food when all of a sudden, he looked at me sternly and said as he stormed out of the house, "Stop judging me! Stop judging me! You are judging me!".

I was left in the house with my mouth hanging open, trying to say, "No, I'm not!" as I was totally confused why he was feeling like this.

It was pouring cats and dogs outside, and the kids were playing in their rooms. So I ran outside after Paul to see what was happening.

*Paul*

I felt so judged. It's the most disturbing feeling I'd ever experienced. So when I ran outside, there was a white dove on the ground on the side of our garage. Mind you, it's pouring, and there are no doves in our neighborhood. Crows, maybe, but no doves. This white dove looks at me and flies to a nearby branch, and I put my hands out and shout, "Wait, don't go!"

"That's it, I'm losing it! Yes, my mind. I'm talking to a bird in the pouring rain in New England of late September."

*Tara*

When I went out after Paul, he was standing on the side of our house next to our garage with his head down and sobbing.

I stood in front of him, picked his head up to look him in the eyes, and asked, "Tell me the truth—did you do what you were accused of?"

He gave me a nod with his head, saying yes.

My eyes locked with his, and I said, "This is the man I can love. This broken man is the man I can love."

*Paul*

I cried so much and out loud, shaking and sniffling. Tara consoled me with the warmest hug. She held me so tight. I could feel "this love" that was comforting, cleansing, accepting, and then I heard—*coooh-coooh...coooh-coooh...*

"What is that?" I asked.

As I moved Tara back from our embrace, the white dove had returned and was walking around her feet. It walked around her feet three times. I just watched with my jaw open to the ground and thought, *What is happening right now? How is this woman whom I not only betrayed but lied to emphatically "consoling me"? I feel this love that I have never felt toward me ever.*

We stood completely still and watched as we were amazed and dumbfounded, because we knew something indescribable just happened. A miracle!

*Tara*

We went back in the house. The rest of the night was a very quiet blur.

I couldn't wait to call Uncle Don and tell him how God was showing up! After sharing with him on the phone, he asked to talk with Paul. They chatted for a while, and Paul handed me the phone to finish the conversation with Don.

Uncle Don said, "Peanut, it is time for me to come and visit. Do you have a place for me to sleep? I will stay as long as the Lord Jesus needs me to."

I said, "Yes…we have a camper in the driveway you can call your own as long as you need."

Uncle Don parked his semitruck in Alabama and borrowed a friend's car to drive to Massachusetts. He filled the trunk with Bibles and concordances (a Bible dictionary) and headed our way. I had no clue what this adventure had in store for us.

The first full day, he spent with us began with Paul showing him the camper and helping him get settled.

*Paul's turning point*

Uncle Don really liked the camper. It was a thirty-six-foot Winnebago with a tag axle. It was a front engine job that we drove all over New England. We sat in the living room, and I could feel that same warm feeling that I felt when the dove was around, and Uncle Don said, "Paul, I'm going to ask you a question. Do you want to give your heart to Jesus?"

Instantly, this huge flood of emotions flowed through me, and it felt like a freight train and a flower garden all at the same time. I wasn't thinking about our marriage, our kids, my sexual addictions, my business, or anything else. I somehow knew that this Jesus was the only answer to everything.

"Yes, Uncle Don. I'm ready"

He said as he led me in a simple prayer, "Repeat after me."

"Jesus, I know that I'm a sinner, that you came to take my sins away. I ask you to forgive my sin and come and live in my heart. Guide me as I walk in this new life. Amen."

I could feel this amazing love fill my heart! It was the same love I saw in my wife over the last week when she looked at me. I could see Jesus in her and Uncle Don, and now I could feel *him* living inside of me.

*Tara*

I quickly brewed some coffee and started to walk out toward the camper with a tray of coffee and snacks. As I was approaching, I saw through the window of the camper that Paul was knelt down at the table with his head down, weeping.

I quickly turned around and headed back to the house. I thought to myself, "Wow. Uncle Don didn't waste any time! My husband was ripe to receive Jesus in his heart! What a miracle!"

Later that night, Don started to teach us how to read the Bible. He had us start in the book of Daniel in the Old testament. It was hard to understand, and reading out loud was intimidating to Paul because he could barely read at all.

When it was time for Paul to take a turn to read, he pleaded. "Uncle Don, please pass me on the reading. It is embarrassing to say this, but... I can't read."

Tears started to fall down Paul's face, and Uncle Don quickly made light of it and said, "That's okay. Nothing is too hard for Jesus."

He stood up and walked over to Paul and put a gentle hand on his shoulder as he prayed, "Lord Jesus, would you help Paul to be able to read your Word? We know that it is not too hard for you!"

Paul looked down at the page and started to read the book of Daniel. He was amazed that he could read without a struggle, and the tears came flowing down his face again with joy. Another miracle!

Our hearts burned inside of us as we read the Scriptures with Uncle Don! We could not get enough! The next day, Paul had to go to work at his auto repair shop, but he came home for lunch because he didn't want to miss out on time with Uncle Don. Paul walked into the kitchen like he was on a mission, opened the fridge to grab some sandwich meat, and offered to make sandwiches for us. However, Uncle Don and I had been talking about my son, Josh, and how he was tormented with nervous ticks (Tourette's Syndrome). My uncle explained to me that Jesus still heals today. The night before, he had us watch the movie, *Jesus of Nazareth*, to help us understand who Jesus is and what he does. Therefore, Uncle Don suggested that we fast and pray for three days for Josh to be healed. Therefore, we replied to Paul's offer for sandwiches with, "No, thank you!"

Paul looked confused and said, "Did you already eat?"

We said, "We're fasting."

"What is fasting?"

He said, "It means you don't eat and believe that God, and his word will fill you, and as you pray, you'll see miracles happen."

I said, "For how long?"

"Three days," he replied with total confidence.

I said, "If you don't eat for three days, you'll die."

"No. We are going to fast for three days for Josh to be healed."

"You mean you are not going to eat for three days? How is that possible?" Paul asked.

Uncle Don kindly replied, "Don't worry. You don't have to join us. Go ahead and have lunch. It's okay."

"Whatever!" Paul spouted as he threw the meat back into the fridge, "If you can do it, I can do it!"

For the next three days, we skipped meals and read the Bible morning, noon, and night, along with prayers for Josh. Uncle Don had explained to us that when you fast, the Bible says to wash your face and anoint your head with oil as well as keeping your countenance in a normal state.

The Bible also says to keep it to yourself and God, otherwise you will not have his reward. In other words, don't brag about it or act like you are making such a sacrifice and appearing down cast. If you do, it will be your only reward.

On the third day, the three of us walked upstairs to Josh's room where he was hanging out. Uncle Don proceeded to share with Josh about the love of Jesus and how he wants to be a friend to him. He asked Josh if he wanted to be God's friend and to invite him to live in his heart, and he nodded his head and said yes!

Don prayed, and Josh repeated after him something like this, "Dear Lord, I believe you sent Jesus to be my savior and friend. Please forgive me for my sins and be my friend as you live in my heart. In Jesus's name, amen."

We could all feel the peace that entered the room. Uncle Don explained to Josh that Jesus is our healer and that we believe he wants to take away the nervous ticks.

"Is it okay for us to pray for Jesus to heal you?"

"Yes!" Josh said with a hopeful grin on his face.

We put our hands on his head gently, and Uncle Don prayed, "In the name of Jesus, we agree that you are the healer, and Josh is your child. So we ask that all nervous ticks be removed from him and be filled with your peace! Amen."

I immediately went downstairs and, by faith, threw his medicine away.

The next few days, we continued to read the Bible with Uncle Don and thanked God for healing our son. I did not see any nervous ticks happening since our prayer, and I was flying high in the fact that God is real, and his Words are alive!

During the day, Paul would go to work, and Uncle Don and I would take Rachel with us on daily errands. The presence of God was so tangible just from talking about Jesus as we went about the day. I felt like I was high on drugs or something. It was pure joy!

*Paul*

I couldn't wait to get home from work and hang out with uncle Don and read the Bible. I wasn't so worried at work anymore or thinking about all the chaos and changes. I was really filled with God's peace. And I could read!

Now came the time to say goodbye to Uncle Don as he had to go back to work. It was hard to see him go but we knew that he was a phone call away, and that we had Jesus!

The next adventure was to find a church, get baptized, and to tell others about Jesus! We looked in the yellow pages for churches and started to call them to ask about baptism.

Uncle Don said, "If they make you go through a class or wait for a specific date, don't go there. You want a pastor who understands if you desire to be baptized, then just do it!" Nobody was calling back after we had left messages at a few churches in the area, so we decided to wait on the Lord about it.

Meanwhile, Uncle Don took us to the streets and demonstrated to us how to say the name of Jesus in conversation with others. First, he said to us, "Say the name of Jesus out loud."

"Jesus," we both said awkwardly.

"Don't be ashamed of that name. Just keep saying his name out loud. Jesus." He repeated.

We kept repeating, "Jesus, Jesus, Jesus," until it began to feel normal as if we were talking about our friend.

Uncle Don showed us what it looked like to follow the leading of the Holy Spirit. Walk up to a stranger, start a friendly conversation, and then do whatever the Holy Spirit leads you to do. It might be to give that person a blessing of finances or to pray for them about a situation they have brought up. It was unpredictable, fulfilling, and very exciting to spend a day like this.

After a couple of days passed, Paul had a new customer come to his repair shop for his broken-down Subaru. It was the kind of repair that Paul hated doing, but his employee booked it. As Paul was looking underneath the car, the customer was standing by the car, and Paul asked him how he found his shop.

The man said, "Oh, I am the pastor of a church right down the street from here, and so I thought I would give you a try."

Paul slid out from underneath the car and said, "What? Really? What kind of church?"

"A Christian storefront church called Victory Chapel"

Paul said, "I have never seen it before. My wife and I just received Jesus as our personal savior, and we desperately want to get baptized. Could you do that for us?"

*Tara*

He just stood there in shock for a second and then said, "Well, yes! Of course!"

Paul added with excitement, "Could you do it this weekend?"

The pastor thought for a second and replied, "We need to find water. Does it matter where?"

Paul asked, "How about the Connecticut River?"

He replied, "It will be cold, but that will do!"

Paul couldn't wait to come home and tell us what the Lord had done. Another miracle! The next Sunday, we all ventured out to try this new church that was right underneath our nose the whole time. It was in a storefront next to a Chinese restaurant where we frequently ordered food. As we entered the building, there were friendly greeters at the door that shook our hands and handed us bulletins. The room was long and narrow with metal folding chairs lined up in rows to sit in. There was a stage area with a big banner on the back wall and equipped with drums, guitars, keyboard, and a pulpit.

The band started playing, and people started clapping and singing with passion. It was overwhelming in a good way. I could feel the presence of the Lord fill up the room. Our children were wide-eyed and clapping along.

He preached a good message that went right to my heart, and I could actually apply to my life. It was very different from our Catholic Church, but I liked it! We all liked it from the start. It was an answer to our prayer, and the next day, we were baptized in the Connecticut River.

Uncle Don's mission was over at this point. He taught us how to feed ourselves by reading the Bible, how to pray, tell others about Jesus, follow the Holy Spirit, and to join a local church family. It was hard to say goodbye, but we were so thankful that he gave us this jumpstart to our new life.

*Paul*

Pastor Jim was a little younger than we were—early thirties, married with two children. He would stop by my repair shop while he was out running errands. He would bring by pizza or sandwiches and just sit and talk to me about life. He was really a good friend and pastor. I love him and so thankful that God brought him into our lives.

# CHAPTER 10

## New Life, New Troubles

I love the scripture in the Bible that says, "Those who are in Christ Jesus are a new creation, the old is gone and all things have become new" (2 Corinthians 5:17).

I did not know what that meant at this time in my life, but God began to show me by experience. For instance, I had been addicted to cigarettes and alcohol since I was a teenager. I had tried to quit many times since then but was only able to stop for the nine months of pregnancy or short three-month spurts.

Drinking alcohol was a must for the weekends, and I wanted at least one beer every night to take the edge off. However, one day after Uncle Don left, I was smoking my usual afternoon cigarette while standing outside in my front yard. As I inhaled, I had a vision of myself wearing a beautiful white wedding dress, and as I exhaled, I saw a dark-yellow stain run down the front of the dress.

I thought to myself, *Yuck. I don't want this!* As I threw the cigarette down on the ground and stomped, it out with my foot. Something miraculous must have happened because I never desired another cigarette after that. It was if I had never smoked.

The same happened with drinking alcohol. I just didn't desire it anymore. A couple of other habits just fell off me which were nail biting and swearing. One day, I noticed that it wasn't happening anymore. I was changing from the inside out, instead of trying to do it by will power. Paul noticed after about a week, that I was not smoking anymore.

*Paul's input.* I had my first cigarette with my friend, Eric, in the woods behind my parent's house at six years old. I started smoking regularly at twelve. I was drinking and using drugs shortly thereafter.

I was hanging out in the living room as he approached me saying, "Hey, I haven't seen you smoke in a while. Did you quit?"

I explained to him what had happened to me, and he said, "Wow! If God can do that for you, then he can do that for me."

He took his pack of cigarettes and knelt down in front of our fireplace and threw them in it as he prayed. "Lord, I ask you to take the desire to smoke away from me, and if I want one, I will call on You to help me. I trust You to do this, and I will tell people how You helped me. In Jesus's name, Amen."

The next challenge of our new life involved telling our friends what had happened to us. We were so excited about Jesus and wanted everyone we knew to know him.

It was early October and the Oxbow Water Ski Team was putting on their annual haunted hayride fundraiser. One of the members called Paul to see if he could volunteer again. Paul answered, saying, "Hey. I'm sorry, but I won't be able to help with that."

"Aw, man! You are the best at getting people into character and scaring people. Can I ask why?"

"Yeah. It's hard to explain, but I have made a decision to follow Jesus, so the haunted hayride does not fit that decision."

"Oh, I see. Well, I highly respect that you follow your convictions. I'm sure that is not easy, and a lot of people don't stand strong in them. So I highly respect that."

"Well, thank you for saying that," Paul stated. We were both sad that we couldn't help them, but we knew we did the right thing.

The following weekend, a couple of Paul's water ski buddies gave Paul a surprise visit to his shop with a six pack of beer in their hands.

"Hey, bro!" They shouted. "What's been happening with you?"

Paul with a surprised look on his face, wiped off his hands, and gave them a hug. "What a surprise!" Paul said with joy.

"We wanted to find out about this change that has happened to you!" They claimed as they handed Paul a beer.

"No thanks. I stopped drinking," Paul said with a smile.

"Are you and Tara okay?" they asked with a concerned look on their faces.

"Yes, but we almost got divorced. It's a long story, but it brought us to Jesus. You don't have to worry that I'm in some cult or something. We both want to serve him, and he has changed our desires."

"Yeah, I used to belong to a Southern Baptist Church. I know about Jesus." One of them claimed. Soon they were convinced that Paul was all right, so they took their last swig of beer and said their goodbyes.

In this new life, we were soon feeling stressed about our finances. We had so many debts and it felt like we were living from paycheck to paycheck. Since we knew we were not going to be joining the waterski club again, the boat was the first debt that needed to go.

The boat was thirteen years old and still had two years to go on the loan. This was a very difficult decision for Paul, but he knew it had to go for more reasons than one. Boating had been in Paul's life since he was five years old and had become something he kind of worshipped. However, God has won Paul's heart at this time, so he gave it up.

The boat sold quickly to a young man in his twenties, and I still remember the look on Paul's face as the boat left the parking lot of his shop. It was pretty emotional for him.

A few hours later, right after Paul showed me the wad of cash that the young man gave him, the phone rang. It was the young man, and he was sobbing frantically as he explained that the trailer came off of the hitch while he was heading home. The boat and trailer crashed into a tree off of the road.

Paul responded, "No way! Man, that sucks for you." After he hung up, he told me what happened.

I pleaded with Paul, "We need to give him the money back. You helped him hitch the boat, and it is the right thing to do. Could this be a test from God?"

That evening Paul drove out to the young man's house to retrieve the boat and to give the money back. The young man and

.s girlfriend were dumfounded. They couldn't believe the kindness they were experiencing.

Paul explained with joy, "Jesus has healed my marriage and saved my life. He is the one to thank. Jesus also changed my heart and wants me to give you back your money and take the boat."

*Paul concludes*

That Monday, I called the insurance company and told them the truth about the accident. Lo and behold, they explained that if the title was still in my name, they would pay me for the loss. I didn't realize that I had insured the boat for replacement value. They gave me over $12,000 for the loss after the deductible and loan payoff. I had sold the boat for $4500.

We were amazed with gratitude in our hearts, for we knew God was rewarding us.

Life was moving on. The kids were in fourth and fifth grade. Rachel was in preschool. Thanksgiving break was coming up, and we decided to take a trip to Arizona to visit my dad. Meeting my dad in Wisconsin at the reunion was awesome, but I wanted to get to know him better. He was quiet like me, and I knew one on one time would be beneficial for our relationship.

We owned a class A motorhome and loved to drive cross-country. The kids took some extra time off school so we had schoolwork to do along the way. They loved doing their work, sitting at the dining table while watching the world go by.

Unfortunately, we had some engine trouble by the time we were in Pennsylvania. Paul saw white smoke coming from the engine. We pulled off the side of the road, opened the hood, and saw that the head gasket was cracked. It was funny because we were listening to a new CD by Ron Kenoly called God Is Able. So he shut the hood of the engine and decided to sing. "God is able to do what he said he would do." Every time we saw smoke, we sang those words. We made it all the way to Arizona!

This was a mechanical impossibility! The water didn't run low, and the engine didn't overheat. A miracle.

My dad lived in Flagstaff, which is right near the Grand Canyon. His house was beautiful and had lots of acreage with dogs and horses. It was a dream home for our kids because they loved animals. This was a dream come true for me because I was having Thanksgiving with my dad and his family.

After spending three days together, sightseeing and hanging out, it was time to head back home. The winds were fierce going through the Midwest. It was so exhausting just trying to keep the motorhome on the road. We had to pull off the road a couple of times to fix the awning. I should have known that it was a sign of conflict coming our way.

As we were heading near Indiana, Paul thought it would be nice to stop and visit my parents and to let Josh visit his dad for an evening.

"Give your mom a call and let her know we are stopping by," Paul suggested with a smile.

I said, "Oh, that's a great idea! Josh would love that!"

My mom answered the phone, and I said, "Hey, Mom, how was your Thanksgiving?"

"It was fine. How was your trip?" she asked.

"It was great. We had a blast, and we got to see the Grand Canyon! Hey, Mom, we are almost in Indiana, and Paul thought it would be fun to stop by for a visit if you are up to it."

She all of a sudden had a high-pitched tone to her voice that sounded so fake and said, "Okay, that would be nice. What time do you think you will be here?"

"Um…we should be there in two hours."

After the call ended, I expressed to Paul, "Something is up. My mom sounded so strange. I have a weird feeling in my stomach!"

A few hours later, we pulled up in my parent's driveway. Josh's dad was already there waiting to pick him up for a visit. We stretched our legs and gathered some belongings before we stepped out of the motorhome. Sam came walking over to greet us, and as he was standing in the driveway, I noticed he was shaking. His legs, arms, and hands were vibrating, and he seemed so distracted. I thought it was weird but didn't mention it. After Josh left with his dad, we headed in the house.

My parents greeted us with the usual small talk and led Kaeley and Rachel to the play room. They summoned Paul and I to the living room to have a talk. I sat next to my stepdad on the sofa. My mom sat in a chair, and Paul sat in a chair across from her.

My mom looked at Paul with a very serious face and said, "My daughter has told me that she is born again because there was a crisis in your marriage. What do you have to say about that?"

"Well… I am born again too. The crisis brought us both to Jesus!" he said humbly.

She responded with, "Well, how do I know it's for real? You don't seem to be very contrite about it!"

"What do you expect me to do? Grovel on the floor? I'm pretty excited about my new salvation and heart change. I'm filled with God's peace and love, and our marriage is really a miracle."

At this point, I was feeling the judgement and the horrible vibes in the room.

The next statement from my mom shocked me. "I believe that you abused Josh. As a matter of fact, Sam believes it too, so he is not bringing Josh back to you!"

"I have purchased a gun and I have been practicing shooting! It is in my closet, and I plan to blow your f——ing head off!"

My jaw hit the floor, and I couldn't even breathe at this point. I turned to look at my stepdad's reaction, and he had a blank stare on his face. I thought to myself, *Who are these people? Who snatched their bodies?*

Paul looked her straight in the eyes, plopped his Bible on the floor, and knelt down on it.

Then he professed, "Go ahead. Get your gun and shoot. One of two things are going to happen, either you will kill me, and I will meet Jesus, or you won't be able to get off of that chair to shoot your gun."

Sure enough, she was trying to stand up to get the gun, and she couldn't physically get up.

I ran to the phone to call Sam to see if it was true. He confirmed that they conspired to keep Josh and were going to fight this together in court. As I became hysterical, I hung up the phone.

I heard the Lord's still small voice say, "This battle is not yours, do not fight this in the natural. It will only cause more harm. This battle belongs to me. Just go home and fight on your knees!"

God's peace came over me immediately so heavy that it felt like a thick blanket all around me. I felt like I was on muscle relaxers as I told Paul what had happened. He was not in agreement at first. He wanted to charge right over to Sam's house and get our boy, but I pleaded with him to trust God.

We grabbed Rachel and Kaeley and stormed out of their house. The ride home was difficult, but I still had God's tangible peace all over me. All that I could do was pray and sing worship songs.

The reality of what had happened started to surface as we were back home, trying to move forward. It was now the Christmas season, and my world was in shambles. I felt depressed. I didn't want to hear the Christmas carols or joyful music of the season. Just getting off the couch seemed impossible.

God was my stronghold. I kept on reading the Bible because that was the only time I could breathe in and out. I didn't go to church for a couple of weeks because I didn't want to be a puddle of tears. Paul did all of the Christmas shopping because I didn't want to leave the house.

Finally, the week before Christmas, I made myself go to church. We had a special speaker preach that day, and I will never forget that message. The title was "Choose Joy!" I had a revelation that day that joy was a choice not a feeling. After the message he called people up to the alter to choose joy, and I ran.

I cried my eyeballs out as I told God, "I want to choose joy no matter what!"

After I stood up, the depression was gone.

*Paul's perspective*

My anger, however, was not gone. I want our son back, and I want them to pay for this. I fantasized about using my 306 from far away enough to not get caught. Maybe borrow a car so that I had an alibi. I couldn't even worship. I knew that there was a great wall that

I had put up and that I couldn't break through it. It was a wall of unforgiveness toward my in-laws and Sam.

I would go to the church every morning for prayer before work, and one day, I heard the Lord say to me, "Pray for them." I thought, *Pray for them? Are you kidding? After what they did to us and accused me of?*

"But, God, I love you more than I hate them and if that's what *you* want, I'll do it."

I prayed, "Bless them and the whole gang involved in this thing." Immediately, I broke down in tears. The anger was gone, and I had the love of God for them, so I prayed for them daily.

*Tara*

I overheard a young couple talking about the fact that they had lost their children in court due to their old life of drug abuse. They were going to have them for a visit for Christmas, but they were sad because they did not have a tree or decorations for their apartment.

I whispered in Paul's ear, "Let's give them our tree in the attic and our old decorations."

He agreed. Immediately we left the church and grabbed our stuff from the attic and helped them decorate. It was so joyful!

The next day, I drove to the Christian bookstore, looking for a book on prayer. I wanted to be able to fight this battle on my knees, but I wanted it to be the most effective. The Bible has a verse in the book of James, chapter 5, which says, "The earnest prayer of a righteous man has great power and wonderful results." Therefore, I looked in the prayer section of the bookstore, and one stood out to me called *Intercessory Prayer* by Dutch Sheets.

I devoured that book! I began to pray fervently and multiple times daily for Josh, my parents, and Sam. I forgave. I started sending letters daily to my mom with words of encouragement. I also sent letters to Josh reminding him that I love him and that all is okay.

About five and a half months went by, and I will never forget the moment that I felt like all of God's patience lifted off me. I was sitting on the toilet in our first-floor bathroom off our kitchen, when all of a sudden, I started to feel an explosive anger rise up inside of me.

I started to yell at God, "Why…why! I don't understand why I have to lose all of my family! Why do I have to be like an orphan! I don't understand. I have given you everything! I serve you day and night! Why do I feel like I'm being punished!"

I started to stomp my feet and wailed like I was having a temper tantrum. After I came to my senses, I left the bathroom, and I heard a knock at the front door. I peered through the window and saw that it was an Express Mail truck. I immediately opened the door and received a thick large envelope with a return address from my parents.

My heart stopped beating, as I thought to myself, *What's this? Custody papers?*

I was afraid to open it, but it had to be done. What I found inside was a six-page apology note from my dad and mom.

They both wrote in their in own words. "Will you forgive me? We meddled in your life, judged Paul, and it was wrong! We know we don't deserve it, but we truly ask you both to forgive us."

I dropped to the floor and cried like a baby. I just got done screaming at God, and I felt so shameful to have lost faith in a most faithful God. He knew this letter was about to arrive. Yet he loves us, and when we think there is no hope, hope is on the way!

*Paul*

Tara immediately called me and said that she had an emergency. I rushed home from the shop and ran into the house and said, "What's wrong? What happened?"

When she showed me the paper, we both cried, worshipped God, and thanked him for his faithfulness. They even wrote a separate page, just to me, asking forgiveness.

*God was not done*

About two days later, Sam called me and said, "Hey… I just wanted to let you know that I am convinced that Paul did not abuse

Josh. After having him here for five months, I realize that he is fine. I told your mother to stop meddling in your life and that I am going to send Josh back to you for the summer."

God did it! He fought the battle and won! No attorneys, no psychologists, and no fighting back and forth! Our part was to forgive before they knew they needed it and to pray fervently. Waiting on the Lord can seem passive, but in reality, he is working mightily!

*In conclusion*

These were first of many battles big and small, but God always helps us walk through them. It is twenty years later from the beginning of this story.

Ultimately, God used my earthly dad to call me into an amazing relationship with my heavenly Father, who has made us royalty and gifted us with an amazing inheritance of love, forgiveness, power, wisdom, reconciliation, eternal life, and so much more through the Holy Spirit!

Paul and I wrote this book for such a time as this. This is a true story about a God who desires relationship with all of us, and if you felt him knock on the door of your heart, let him in by praying, "Dear Lord, if you can do this for Paul and Tara, you can do this for me. I surrender my old life. I desire to put you first, and I desire to truly know you. Fill me with your love for you, myself, and others. Help me to find others to walk with and to share your love with. I trust you. In Jesus's name. Amen."

There are over twenty years of miracles that we have experienced in our family and seen in others, both locally and in other countries. Stay tuned for more.

We pray God's grace and peace be multiplied to you, in Jesus's name! Amen.

# ABOUT THE AUTHOR

T. Marie Spencer is the author of Radical Rescue, an inspirational true story of an ordinary life that becomes extraordinary. Spencer is a wife, a mother, grandmother, and an ordained minister of a community church in New England. Cosmetology was her first occupation before entering full-time ministry. Spencer also has traveled worldwide with her husband as conference speakers, missionaries, and overseers of churches. She loves to encourage and impart hope to women struggling with marriage and parenting.

CPSIA information can be obtained
at www.ICGtesting.com
Printed in the USA
BVHW041648180423
662582BV00004B/131

9 781662 480782